Make It Write RIGHT!

Introductory Level
Proof Reading Activities
Key Stage 1 Age Group 5-8 Years

Photocopiable Masters

Correlated with the Spelling Made Easy
Revised Introductory Level Textbook

Spelling Made Easy

by Ceri Williams

Based on Multi Sensory Structured Phonics Method by Violet Brand

www.spellingmadeeasy.co.uk

Make It Right
Proof Reading Activities
for
Spelling Made Easy Introductory Level
First published in the United Kingdom in 2014
by Ceri Williams
(based on 'Spelling Made Easy' by Violet Brand)

Copyright assigned to Spelling Made Easy Ltd.
Ceri Williams and Violet Brand (2014)

ISBN 978-1-904421-405

All rights reserved. The copymasters contained in this publication are protected by international copyright laws. The copyright of all materials in the 'Spelling Made Easy' series remains the property of the publisher and the author. The publisher hereby grants photocopying rights of this work for use with 'Spelling Made Easy' textbooks. Otherwise, no part of this book may be reproduced or translated in any form or by any means, electronic or mechanical, including recording or by any information storage or retrieval system without permission in writing from the publisher.

CONTENTS

Make It R~~ite~~ W~~ite~~ RIGHT! ✓
Introductory Level

Introduction and Biography

		page	Teaching Points and Cross References page
Activity 1.	Short vowels a,o,e,i,u	2,3	34
Activity 2.	Short vowels a,o,e,i,u	4,5	34
Activity 3.	Consonant Clusters and Phonemes ck,ee,oo,ar,or	6,7	34
Activity 4.	Consonant Clusters and Phonemes ck,ee,oo,ar,or	8,9	34
Activity 5.	Consonant Clusters sh,ch,th	10,11	35
Activity 6.	Consonant Clusters sh,ch,th	12,13	35
Activity 7.	Long Vowels a-e,i-e,o-e,u-e	14,15	35
Activity 8.	Long Vowels a-e,i-e,o-e,u-e	16,17	35
Activity 9.	Vowel Blending ai,oa,ir,ou,ea	18,19	36
Activity 10.	Vowel Blending ai,oa,ir,ou,ea	20,21	36
Activity 11.	Vowel Blending and Endings -ay,-ing,ur,aw,oi	22,23	36
Activity 12.	Vowel Blending and Endings -ay,-ing,ur,aw,oi	24,25	36
Activity 13.	Vowel Blending and Endings er,all,y,ea,ow	26,27	37
Activity 14.	Vowel Blending and Endings er,all,y,ea,ow	28,29	37
Activity 15.	Various igh,a,o,y,ow	30,31	37
Activity 16.	Various igh,a,o,y,ow	32,33	37

Make It ~~Rite~~, ~~Write~~, RIGHT!

Introduction

Proof reading is an essential part of written English – it requires visual scrutiny of the passage as well as comprehension, to spot mistakes. These exercises will hopefully develop pupils' reading and spelling skills through guided and individual completion of the activities.

The mistakes written into the text are mainly, but not exclusively, from all the spelling pattern/word families covered in the relevant Spelling Made Easy Teacher's Textbooks and the accompanying 'Fun With Phonics' and 'Spelling Made Easy At Home' series. The aim is further reinforcement and overlearning of the spelling patterns covered in the programme, as well as common High Frequency Words. In the first two levels, aspects of punctuation are confined to capitals at the beginning of a sentence and proper nouns, full stops (periods), and the odd exclamation mark! Punctuation problems increase in complexity throughout the series but are basic in the first two levels, as a flow to the reading is desirable.

Guidelines

- If required, use the first few exercises and model and share the task with the pupil/s. Proof-reading is a skill that requires practice and tuition.

- Read through the passage for meaning and discuss any arising points.

- Get the pupil to follow the words with a 'special' pen/pencil as they or you are reading it.

- Point out punctuation errors and model how sentences sound without full stops especially.

- Re-read and annotate/identify errors. Again, model and share the tasks, especially with reluctant readers and writers.

As the pupils progress through the activities, their particular areas for possible further revision and consolidation work should become apparent through analysis of their answers and responses during lessons.

Ceri Williams

Hey you! Yes you!
Can you help Make It Right?

wrong spellings

There are lots of rong spellins in these bits of writing. spot

riting. Can you spott them and Make It Right?

some

There are also sume capitals and full stops missing. can

missin See if you kan find them all!

Good luck!

Ceri Williams

Born in Usk, South Wales, Ceri has taught across primary and secondary phases in both mainstream and special schools. He works in the special needs sector in South Wales. His awards include a Microsoft Innovative Teacher Award, an NGFL-Cymru/Microsoft Innovative Teacher Award and The NAACE Impact Award for Inclusion.

Ceri studied music at The Royal Welsh College of Music & Drama, and education at Birmingham University, initially teaching class music. After relocating back to Wales, he began teaching in the special needs sector, completing a Masters in SEN in 2005 at the University of Newport.

He has presented several papers outlining his work in Multimedia Multisensory Environments at international conferences which have been published in academic journals. As well his interests in education, he still performs frequently as a musician.

Introductory Level – Activity 1 – short vowel – 'a', 'e', 'i', 'o', 'u'

A Big Dog

the twins are back ta school. they am upset but mum

and gran are very happy that school has begun agen.

the twinns are ssat on the sfot redd matt inn the class.

at tten past tenn, a bigg doog got onn the yard and

wennt in the binns. it rran to jummp inn the mud, and he

had mudd on hiss leggs. Miss jones wnet nut. sam

and jim were att the buss spot and saw it.

they had a grinn at the badd ddog!

Introductory Level – Activity 1 – short vowel – 'a', 'e', 'i', 'o', 'u'

A Big Dog

The   at   They are   Mum

the twins are back ta school. they am upset but mum

    Gran   again

and gran are very happy that school has begun agen.

The twins   sat   soft red mat in

the twinns are ssat on the sfot redd matt inn the class.

At ten   ten   big dog   on

at tten past tenn, a bigg doog got onn the yard and

went   bins It ran   jump in

wennt in the binns. it rran to jummp inn the mud, and he

    mud   his legs   Jones went nuts Sam

had mudd on hiss leggs. Miss jones wnet nut. sam

    Jim   at   bus stop

and jim were att the buss spot and saw it.

They   grin   bad dog

they had a grinn at the badd ddog!

Introductory Level – Activity 2 – short vowel – 'a', 'e', 'i', 'o', 'u'

Gran's Bags

it was a hhot day. The twins had slepbt late and had to run to school. They had fast leggs! they had been back att school for siks days. They hadd brand new baggs with zipps and new sunn hhats too from gran.

Holly's bbag had a black catt onn it. It was very cool.

Harry's bagg had a foks and a henn on itt.

Harry musst hlep to give out the cupps of mlik at drincks time. It is funn The milkk is in a boks on top of the desk.

Introductory Level – Activity 2 – short vowel – 'a', 'e', 'i', 'o', 'u'

Gran's Bags

It   hot   slept

it was a hhot day. The twins had slepbt late and had to

run   legs They

runn to school. They had fast leggs! they had been back

at   six   had   bags

att school for siks days. They hadd brand new baggs

zips   sun hats   Gran

with zipps and new sunn hhats too from gran.

bag   cat on

Holly's bbag had a black catt onn it. It was very cool.

bag   fox   hen   it

Harry's bagg had a foks and a henn on itt.

must help   cups   milk

Harry musst hlep to give out the cupps of mlik at

drinks   fun.   milk   box

drincks time. It is funn The milkk is in a boks on top of

the desk.

Introductory Level – Activity 3 – 'ck' plus long vowel 'ee', 'oo', 'ar', 'or'

A Good Cook

Dear gran,

we hav had so much hard and triky homework so faar

we get stuk! we have to lok at so many buks we

hardly have any time forr any foowd or fre time to go in

the caar or the parck to meeyt and seee pals.

We can pik sweedcorrn to lik and chees buns

to eat with a fourk. Our mum needs a gud new

coock boook. We keepe getting sic! We don't get to

slep until it goes darc and the moown and starrs are out.

Love, Harry and Holly.

Introductory Level – Activity 3 – 'ck' plus long vowel 'ee', 'oo', 'ar', 'or'

A Good Cook

      Gran

Dear gran,

We have   tricky   far

we hav had so much hard and triky homework so faar

     stuck We   look   books

we get stuk! we have to lok at so many buks we

       for   food   free

hardly have any time forr any foowd or fre time to go in

   car   park   meet   see

the caar or the parck to meeyt and seee pals.

    pick sweetcorn   lick   cheese

We can pik sweedcorrn to lik and chees buns

     fork   good

to eat with a fourk. Our mum needs a gud new

cook   book   keep   sick

coock boook. We keepe getting sic! We don't get to

sleep   dark   moon   stars

slep until it goes darc and the moown and starrs are out.

Love, Harry and Holly.

Introductory Level – Activity 4 – 'ck' plus long vowel 'ee', 'oo', 'ar', 'or'

Sticky Tart

sam met Ann at teh zoow. She had her new grene skarf on. It was three to get in the zooe as the quee was there loking at the brand new treez. At the cake shop, ann lickd her tarrt, she didn't use a spoom. Sown, her skarf went in the jamm jaar an made her neeck stiky. sam laughed so hardd he put hs bak out then hurt his foott He hat to miss the spoort at the parc as he was stuuk in bed

Introductory Level – Activity 4 – 'ck' plus long vowel 'ee', 'oo', 'ar', 'or'

Sticky Tart

Sam   the zoo   green scarf

sam met Ann at teh zoow. She had her new grene skarf

       free   zoo   queen

on. It was three to get in the zooe as the quee was

       looking   trees

there loking at the brand new treez. At the cake shop,

Ann licked   tart   spoon   Soon

ann lickd her tarrt, she didn't use a spoom. Sown, her

scarf   jam   jar   and   neck sticky

skarf went in the jamm jaar an made her neeck stiky.

Sam   hard   his back

sam laughed so hardd he put hs bak out then hurt his

foot.   had   sport   park

foott He hat to miss the spoort at the parc as he was

stuck   ! (or full stop .)

stuuk in bed

Introductory Level – Extension Activity 5 – 'sh', 'ch', 'th'

Fish and Chips

sam wos so luking forward to fis and chipps for luch but

the sop was sut. Sum crooks had pinced the chip-fryers

so they could not sell any fich and ships!

sam had nothing to munnch for his lungch.

"I will be getting thinn!" he said. He chekd teh time. It

was tree o'clok. he got some chiken from the butcher

thhen made some fick cips. It was a yummy lunc

but he did eat it a bitt late.

Introductory Level – Extension Activity 5 – 'sh', 'ch', 'th'

Fish and Chips

Sam was   looking   fish   chips   lunch
sam wos so luking forward to fis and chipps for luch but
    shop   shut Some   pinched
the sop was sut. Sum crooks had pinced the chip-fryers
                        fish   chips
so they could not sell any fich and ships!
Sam   munch   lunch
sam had nothing to munnch for his lungch.
                thin   checked the
"I will be getting thinn!" he said. He chekd teh time. It
     three clock He   chicken
was tree o'clok. he got some chiken from the butcher
then   thick chips   lunch
thhen made some fick cips. It was a yummy lunc
            bit
but he did eat it a bitt late.

Introductory Level – Activity 6 – 'sh', 'ch', 'th'

The March

jim was in a rus to see sam to say a band was on a mach in the parc.

the band played a marc sam liked very mucch called 'Sarp Shot'. a shep from the park mrket had got out and it marched witth te band. it made thhem marrch very badly out ov step. People smiled. After the mmarch thay all had a glass of punc and a chatt.

"I wissh to tank thhat shee for te fun," Jim said.

Introductory Level – Activity 6 – 'sh', 'ch', 'th'

The March

Jim   rush   Sam
jim was in a rus to see sam to say a band was on a
march   park
mach in the parc.
The   march Sam   much
the band played a marc sam liked very mucch
   'Sharp Shot' A sheep   market
called 'Sarp Shot'. a shep from the park mrket had got
      with the   It   them   march
out and it marched witth te band. it made thhem marrch
      of   march
very badly out ov step. People smiled. After the mmarch
they   punch   chat
thay all had a glass of punc and a chatt.
  wish thank that sheep the
"I wissh to tank thhat shee for te fun," Jim said.

Introductory Level – Activity 7 – long vowels – 'a-e', 'i-e', 'o-e', 'u-e'

The Prize Case

Sam went in a bikke rase. He wun first prise and a cup.

he browke the rekcord race tiyme on his bluue biyke.

He madde a hhuge case out of woooud for the prize cupp

so he culd put it in his hom He yused his playne toole to

mayke the wood the right shaype.

He usd fiyve tubbes of gluue to stik the wood.

The cayse fell on his tooe and brroke a bonne! Owww!

Introductory Level – Activity 7 – long vowels – 'a-e', 'i-e', 'o-e', 'u-e'

The Prize Case

        bike race   won   prize

Sam went in a bikke rase. He wun first prise and a cup.

He broke   record   time   blue bike

he browke the rekcord race tiyme on his bluue biyke.

    made   huge   wood   prize cup

He madde a hhuge case out of woooud for the prize cupp

    could   home.   used   plane tool

so he culd put it in his hom He yused his playne toole to

make   shape

mayke the wood the right shaype.

    used five tubes   glue   stick

He usd fiyve tubbes of gluue to stik the wood.

    case   toe   broke   bone

The cayse fell on his tooe and brroke a bonne! Owww!

Introductory Level – Activity 8 – long vowels – 'a-e', 'i-e', 'o-e', 'u-e'

Cake and Smoke

ann is the nam of jim's wif. It is no jowke, she is gud at making ace cakkes. June is Ann's frend. She likes puting the icse frostin on Ann's caks. last week, Ann had to sayve a cak from turning into smok. she had left it in the kooker too long. Her nowse smelled it burning.

Ann said some ruwde words, truue! Junne had a tiny bbite from the siide and it tassted OK.

Sh iyced the kake on the plat.

Introductory Level – Activity 8 – long vowels – 'a-e', 'i-e', 'o-e', 'u-e'

Cake and Smoke

Ann   name   Jim's wife   joke   good

ann is the nam of jim's wif. It is no jowke, she is gud at

       cakes   friend   putting

making ace cakkes. June is Ann's frend. She likes puting

   ice frosting   cakes Last

the icse frostin on Ann's caks. last week, Ann had to

save   cake   smoke She

sayve a cak from turning into smok. she had left it in the

cooker   nose

kooker too long. Her nowse smelled it burning.

       rude   true   June

Ann said some ruwde words, truue! Junne had a tiny

bite   side   tasted

bbite from the siide and it tassted OK.

She iced   cake   plate

Sh iyced the kake on the plat.

Introductory Level – Activity 9 – vowel blending – 'ai', 'oa', 'ir', 'ou', 'ea'(ee)

Paint and Dirt

sam looked ouwt at the raiyn clouds as he had his tost and teea. he made a lloud growan as he put his shrit on.

he had to put a new cot of pant on the traine at the raill trak frist, he had to cleen the dirrt off. After the dirtt was cleand off, sam took a seet and had more tee. later, he did a loud groane agen. He had got pint on his shrirt!

Introductory Level – Activity 9 – vowel blending – 'ai', 'oa', 'ir', 'ou', 'ea'(ee)

Paint and Dirt

Sam   out   rain   toast
sam looked ouwt at the raiyn clouds as he had his tost
    tea   He   loud   groan   shirt
and teea. he made a lloud growan as he put his shrit on.
He   coat   paint   train
he had to put a new cot of pant on the traine at the
rail track. First,   clean   dirt   dirt
raill trak frist, he had to cleen the dirrt off. After the dirtt
   cleaned   Sam   seat   tea Later
was cleand off, sam took a seet and had more tee. later,
    groan again   paint   shirt
he did a loud groane agen. He had got pint on his shrirt!

Introductory Level – Activity 10 – vowel blending – 'ai', 'oa', 'ir', 'ou', 'ea'(ee)

Food Fix

a mousse had a paine around his waistt and in his taail.

he had etaen a snairl he had fund in a boatt down the

rode by the seea. a girl shoated at a birrd who nearly

took the mouse. she gave the mouse some meet,

peass, bans and crream to makke the paiin go.

she gave the mouse a wash in her hous with some

soup. the mous used the girl's sckirt to get dry

and the pan went.

Introductory Level – Activity 10 – vowel blending – 'ai', 'oa', 'ir', 'ou', 'ea'(ee)

Food Fix

A mouse   pain   waist   tail
a mousse had a paine around his waistt and in his taail.
He   eaten   snail   found   boat
he had etaen a snairl he had fund in a boatt down the
road   sea   A   shouted   bird
rode by the seea. a girl shoated at a birrd who nearly
                 She   meat
took the mouse. she gave the mouse some meet,
peas   beans   cream   make   pain
peass, bans and crream to makke the paiin go.
She   house
she gave the mouse a wash in her hous with some
soap The mouse   skirt
soup. the mous used the girl's sckirt to get dry
      pain
and the pan went.

Introductory Level – Activity 11 – 'ay', ing', 'ur', 'aw', 'oi'

Well Played

it was Tusday. sam had been sleepng and awoke with a yown. He crauls out of bed and drarws the cuurtains. He forgot gran was comign to saty. She was staing until Thusday. Sam went down to joyn gran. sam saw Gran was cookig a joynt of beef. gran was at boling poin because it was startig to bun! Sam said to turnn the joinnt. The jont didn't buurn.

Gran said, "Well playd Sam!"

Introductory Level – Activity 11 – 'ay', 'ing', 'ur', 'aw', 'oi'

Well Played

It   Tuesday Sam   sleeping
it was Tusday. sam had been sleepng and awoke with a
yawn   crawls   draws   curtains
yown. He crauls out of bed and drarws the cuurtains. He
    Gran   coming   stay   staying
forgot gran was comign to saty. She was staing until
Thursday   join Gran Sam
Thusday. Sam went down to joyn gran. sam saw Gran
  cooking joint   Gran   boiling point
was cookig a joynt of beef. gran was at boling poin
      starting burn   turn
because it was startig to bun! Sam said to turnn the
joint   joint   burn
joinnt. The jont didn't buurn.
        played
Gran said, "Well playd Sam!"

Introductory Level – Activity 12 – 'ay', ing', 'ur', 'aw', 'oi'

Holiday Noise

jim and ann went awway on holday on satuday in the

kar. Wen ann went off to payy for the parkig, jim

checked the ooil as there woz a nois comig from the car.

ann came back, as she needed cons for the parkin.

Thay were standing on a grassy larwn lookig at a nice

churc. a wild durkey came flyin in low and hurrt sam's

jjaw with its claww! Sam made a loud nose!

ann's jaww hit the floor!

Introductory Level – Activity 12 – 'ay', 'ing', 'ur', 'aw', 'oi'

Holiday Noise

Jim   Ann   away   holiday   Saturday

jim and ann went awway on holday on satuday in the

car   When Ann   pay   parking Jim

kar. Wen ann went off to payy for the parkig, jim

    oil   was noise coming

checked the ooil as there woz a nois comig from the car.

Ann   coins   parking

ann came back, as she needed cons for the parkin.

They   lawn looking

Thay were standing on a grassy larwn lookig at a nice

church A   turkey   flying   hurt Sam's

churc. a wild durkey came flyin in low and hurrt sam's

jaw   claw   noise

jjaw with its claww! Sam made a loud nose!

Ann's jaw

ann's jaww hit the floor!

Introductory Level – Activity 13 – 'er', all', 'y', 'ea', 'ow'

Summer and Winter

it wos Novmber. gran had called by and sam and gran were sittig dowun al cosy by the fireplace in the wal.

"It seems like only yestaday it was summar," said sam.

Gran was grumpe. She sed, "It's windey, mistee and frostiy nnow, howw it's getting me dowwn!"

Sam sed he'd red the paper and that hevy rain was going to fall instad of the frostey, missty weather. Gran was even more grumpee.

Introductory Level – Activity 13 – 'er', 'all', 'y', 'ea', 'ow'

Summer and Winter

It was November Gran   Sam   Gran
it wos Novmber. gran had called by and sam and gran
   sitting down all   wall
were sittig dowun al cosy by the fireplace in the wal.
              yesterday   summer   Sam
"It seems like only yestaday it was summar," said sam.
        grumpy   said   windy   misty
Gran was grumpe. She sed, "It's windey, mistee and
frosty now, how   down
frostiy nnow, howw it's getting me dowwn!"
   said   read   heavy
Sam sed he'd red the paper and that hevy rain was
     instead   frosty   misty
going to fall instad of the frostey, missty weather. Gran
     grumpy
was even more grumpee.

Introductory Level – Activity 14 – 'er', all', 'y', 'ea', 'ow'

The Town Hall Ball

ann and jim were going to the bawll at the towwn horll as they had had a leter to invite them. "Shall we have dinnur earley or have a late suppar?" ann asked.

Jim said, "Let's get redy and get to townn for tweny past seven, there will be a good croawd there. Thern we can hed back earlee and have a late super."

Ann said, "Yes, we can have pleny of cruste brawn bred with cheese spraed and a smal cup of milke coffee."

Jim said "Yum!"

Introductory Level – Activity 14 – 'er', all', 'y', 'ea', 'ow'

The Town Hall Ball

Ann   Jim   ball   town hall

ann and jim were going to the bawll at the towwn horll as

               letter

they had had a leter to invite them. "Shall we have

dinner early   supper Ann

dinnur earley or have a late suppar?" ann asked.

              ready   town   twenty

Jim said, "Let's get redy and get to townn for tweny past

                   crowd   Then

seven, there will be a good croawd there. Thern we can

head   early   supper

hed back earlee and have a late super."

               plenty   crusty brown bread

Ann said, "Yes, we can have pleny of cruste brawn bred

      spread   small   milky

with cheese spraed and a smal cup of milke coffee."

Jim said "Yum!"

Introductory Level – Activity 15 – 'igh', 'a', 'o', 'y', 'ow'

Snow In The Sky

sam was taking a barth as he was visitng his muther and farther in Lundun that nite. "I hop it stays dri. It mighht snoe toniyt and miy fathr has to flyy on munday," he said, loking out of the frunt windeow at the skiy.

"I would rarther him take the uther fligt when the chancce of sneow is loow."

As he got in the car, sume liht snouw began to fal...

Introductory Level – Activity 15 – 'igh', 'a', 'o', 'y', 'ow'

Snow In The Sky

Sam　　　　　bath　　　　visiting　　mother
sam was taking a barth as he was visitng his muther and
father　　London　　night　　hope　　　dry　　　might
farther in Lundun that nite. "I hop it stays dri. It mighht
snow tonight　　my father　　　　fly　　　Monday
snoe toniyt and miy fathr has to flyy on munday," he
　　looking　　　　　　front window　　　　sky
said, loking out of the frunt windeow at the skiy.
　　　　　rather　　　　　　other flight
"I would rarther him take the uther fligt when the
chance　　snow　　low
chancce of sneow is loow."
　　　　　　　　　　some light snow　　　　fall
As he got in the car, sume liht snouw began to fal...

Introductory Level – Activity 16 – 'igh', a', 'o', 'y', 'ow'

Yellow Lights

it was nearly midnite. The traffic was sloe as the wind had begun to graow and bloww the sneow. the brite ligts of Lundun were a pretty siht. The yelow street lihts glowd. sam went up the parth biy the grarss slowly as it woz like glarss. he did not want a narsty fall.

"Hello sun," sam's farther said. He was fliying off to see his brouther.

"Why are you sad muthr?" said Sam. "Trry not to croy. Dad wil buy you a present." Mum didn't criy.

Introductory Level – Activity 16 – 'igh', a', 'o', 'y', 'ow'

Yellow Lights

<u>It</u>   <u>midnight</u>   <u>slow</u>
it was nearly midnite. The traffic was sloe as the wind
     <u>grow</u>   <u>blow</u>   <u>snow</u> <u>The</u> <u>bright</u>
had begun to graow and bloww the sneow. the brite
<u>lights</u> <u>London</u>   <u>sight</u>   <u>yellow</u>   <u>lights</u>
ligts of Lundun were a pretty siht. The yelow street lihts
<u>glowed</u> <u>Sam</u>   <u>path</u> <u>by</u>   <u>grass</u>
glowd. sam went up the parth biy the grarss slowly
   <u>was</u>   <u>glass</u> <u>He</u>   <u>nasty</u>
as it woz like glarss. he did not want a narsty fall.
   <u>son</u>   <u>Sam's father</u>   <u>flying</u>
"Hello sun," sam's farther said. He was fliying off to see
   <u>brother</u>
his brouther.
       <u>Mother</u>   <u>Try</u>   <u>cry</u>
"Why are you sad muthr?" said Sam. "Trry not to croy.
   <u>will</u>   <u>cry</u>
Dad wil buy you a present." Mum didn't criy.

Teaching points – Page 2

High Frequency Words – the, again, saw, are, and, went, school
Short vowels a, e, i, o, u

Example words from SME books - VB Textbook Intro Level Pages 2-6 FWP Pages 2-5	at	on	in	went	mud
	Sam	dog	Jim	red	up
	ran	stop	big	ten	bus
	bad	soft	his	leg	jump

Teaching points – Page 4

High Frequency Words – they, after, them, give
Short vowels a, e, i, o, u

Example words from SME books - VB Textbook Intro Level Pages 2-6 FWP Pages 2-5	cat	hot	six	leg	cup
	Gran	box	milk	hen	fun
	bag	top	zip	help	sun
	hat	fox	drink	slept	must

Teaching points – Page 6

High Frequency Words – any, many
Consonant clusters and phonemes – 'ck', 'ee', 'oo', 'ar', 'or'

Example words from SME books - VB Textbook Intro Level Pages 7-11 FWP Pages 5-9	sick	see	food	car	fork
	pick	free	moon	far	corn
	stuck	sweet	cook	park	for
	lick	meet	good	dark	

Teaching points – Page 8

High Frequency Words – new, laughed, then, there
Consonant clusters and phonemes – 'ck', 'ee', 'oo', 'ar', 'or'

Example words from SME books - VB Textbook Intro Leve Pages 7-11 FWP Pages 5-9	back	free	zoo	park	fork
	lick	tree	spoon	scarf	for
	stick	green	look	tart	storm
	neck	queen	foot	jar	sport

Teaching points – Page 10

High Frequency Words – for, some, nothing, could
Consonant clusters – 'sh', 'ch', 'th'
'ch' vs. 'tch'
butcher

Example words from SME books - VB Textbook Intro Level Pages 12-14 FWP Pages 10-13	shop	chips	three
	shut	pinch	thin
	fish	chicken	thick
	dish	munch	then

Teaching points – Page 12

High Frequency Words – said, out, the, people
Consonant clusters – 'sh', 'ch', 'th'
*punch – a fruit drink

Example words from SME books - VB Textbook Intro Level Pages 12-14 FWP Pages 10-13	sheep	chat	that
	wish	punch	think
	sharp	much	thank
	rush	march	with

Teaching points – Page 14

High Frequency Words – right, went
'o' making 'u' in 'won'
Long vowels – 'a-e', 'i-e', 'o-e', 'u-e'

Example words from SME books - VB Textbook Intro Level Pages 15-18 FWP Pages 14-17	case	bike	home	blue
	made	prize	broke	glue
	plane	five	toe	tube
	shape	time	bone	huge

Teaching points – Page 16

High Frequency Words – friend, week, too
doubled consonant e.g. put – putting
Long vowels – 'a-e', 'i-e', 'o-e', 'u-e'

Example words from SME books - VB Textbook Intro Level Pages 15-18 FWP Pages 14-17	cake	bite	nose	June
	save	like	joke	true
	plate	wife	smoke	tune
	name	ice	rope	rude

Teaching points – Page 18

Vowel blending – 'ai', 'oa', 'ir', 'ou', 'ea'(ee)

Example words from SME books - VB Textbook Intro Level Pages 19-23 FWP Pages 18-21	rain	coat	shirt	cloud	eat
	train	toast	dirt	out	tea
	rail	groan	first	round	seat
	paint	float		loud	dream

Teaching points – Page 20

High Frequency Words – nearly, some, around
Vowel blending – 'ai', 'oa', 'ir', 'ou', 'ea'(ee)

Example words from SME books - VB Textbook Intro Level Pages 19-23 FWP Pages 18-21	pain	boat	skirt	found	meat
	tail	road	girl	shout	peas
	snail	loaf	bird	house	beans
	waist	soap		mouse	cream

Teaching points – Page 22

High Frequency Words – Tuesday, coming, with, saw
curtains – 'ai' sounding as short 'i'
Vowel blending and endings – 'ay', ing', 'ur', 'aw', 'oi'

Example words from SME books - VB Textbook Intro Level Pages 24-28 FWP Pages 22-25	play	playing	burn	yawn	point
	day	sleeping	Thursday	saw	join
	stay	staying	burst	draw	boil
	Tuesday	cooking	turn	crawl	

Teaching points – Page 24

Rhyming – 'jaw' and 'floor'
Vowel blending and endings – 'ay', ing', 'ur', 'aw', 'oi'

Example words from SME books- VB Textbook Intro Level Pages 24-28 FWP Pages 22-25	pay	looking	church	lawn	coin
	holiday	helping	Saturday	jaw	oil
	away	parking	turkey	claw	noise
	Sunday	standing	hurt	saw	

Teaching points – Page 26

'fireplace' – compound words
Vowel blending and endings – 'er', 'all', 'y', 'ea', 'ow'

Example words from SME books - VB Textbook Intro Level Pages 29-33 FWP Pages 26-29	November	all	windy	heavy	down
	winter	wall	misty	read	now
	summer	call	frosty	instead	how
	yesterday	fall	grumpy	ready	

Teaching points – Page 28

High Frequency Words – were, said
Vowel blending and endings – 'er', 'all', 'y', 'ea', 'ow'

Example words from SME books - VB Textbook Intro Level Pages 29-33 FWP Pages 26-29	dinner	ball	crusty	head	town
	supper	tall	plenty	ready	crowd
	letter	hall	milky	spread	brown
	under	small	twenty	bread	

Teaching points – Page 30

High Frequency Words – was, when, began
Mnemonics for 'ight' words – e.g. **I**'ve **g**ot **h**ot **t**oast
… – the ellipsis indicating something unfinished
Various – 'igh', 'a', 'o', 'y', 'ow'

Example words from SME books - VB Textbook Intro Level Pages 34-38 FWP Pages 30-33	light	bath	other	fly	low
	night	last	London	dry	window
	tonight	rather	front	my	snow
	might	father	Monday	sky	

Teaching points – Page 32

High Frequency Words- – nearly, begun, want
Mnemonics for 'ight' words – e.g. **I**'ve **g**ot **h**ot **t**oast
'by' and 'buy'
Various – 'igh', 'a', 'o', 'y', 'ow'

Example words from SME books- VB Textbook Intro Level Pages 34-38 FWP Pages 30-33	midnight	path	son	why	grow
	sight	nasty	brother	cry	slow
	right	grass	mother	by	blow
	bright	glass		try	yellow